Unapologetic Poetic Speaking

Shameeka Williams

ISBN: 978-0-9984626-0-8

First published by Shameeka Williams in 2018

Copyright © Shameeka Williams, 2018

All rights reserved.
No part of this publication may be reproduced,
stored, or transmitted in any form or by any means,
electronic,
mechanical, photocopying, recording, scanning, or
otherwise
without written permission from the publisher.
It is illegal to copy
this book, post it to a website, or distribute it by any
other means
without permission.

To Those who have been there
without being asked,
Who Loved without being forced,
Who embraced without judgement
Thank You
From the Bottom of My Heart

CONTENTS

Ode to Maya Angelou
Pardon My Poetry
Koncrete Jewels
Purpose
Ask Wisely
Liars
Round the Table
No Filter
Life Food
One Day
Truth
Reckless Tendencies
Apple Pie & Puffy Eyes
Scorned
Impress Me
Dynamic Duo
The Other Side of Visitation
All Aboard
What If
Dying for The Wrong Shit
Be Better
For My People
C.R.A.C.K

~Ode to Maya Angelou~

You Inspired me to accept every flaw
made me question
if they were truly flaws at all
or simply false expectations
put in place by those
so far from perfect
but dying to be
unlike them
I don't want perfect
I just want to be me
some days I'm not a morning person
Some days I'm goofy
The things that make me feel Beautiful
are not for you to understand or see
why must I cover my face
with a shit load of make up
for you to notice me
I don't have insecurities
that's what happens
when you don't have inner peace
My Beauty is my own
Phenomenal in my own lane
With an appreciation that's strong

~Pardon My Poetry~

Pardon my poetry
But this isn't about you
And it isn't about me
It's about those that will come
After we
so we must tend to the seeds
We planted
While the sun still shines
Upon us
Because once the dirt is on us
Those left behind
Will mourn us
But what tools will they have
What knowledge could they share
Did you leave behind a legacy?
Or another burden to bare
Did you teach your seed responsibility?
Or were you also unprepared
Because we cannot give
what we never had
and most of our elders
don't acknowledge their heirs
History has a funny way of repeating
until the mistakes you made are clear
it's not a question how you got here
but what you do with your provided time
most of us use it wisely
while others simply refuse to shine
the sun doesn't appear for nothing
it has important work to do
it provides us with the fuel

we need to move
the tools we need to grow
the warmth we need to show
sad to say some of us are still cold
and grow colder as we grow older
because our childhood went a certain way
but instead of getting the proper healing
we were told to put some shit away
silence created confusion
causing demons to form
fingers began to point
because the actions
are condemned
rather than explained
and mama can't understand your pain
so you never open up again
sad but true
straight facts
so let's change a thing or two
let's raise children who won't need therapy
let's raise children
who follows their dreams
let's raise children
with far less wounds
than we ever knew
let's raise children
better than me and you
let's raise children to see beyond the color
of the next person's skin
teach them to respect life
because before those labels are applied
we are all Humans!!!

~Koncrete Jewels~

Don't let anyone make you feel like
you come from nothing
the lesson is in the struggle
teaches you
how to appreciate
something
when it is earned
not giving
there's a difference
most don't witness
because if you
know privilege
you are not familiar
with struggle
and when you
know struggle
you are condemned
when you hustle
but you're only trying to make it
enjoy it for a lil bit
before they find a way
to take it
sometimes we even
pass it down
likes it sacred
because where I'm from
we're not giving anything
so the mindset is to
take it
then there's some of us

that rather work a 9 to 5
helping someone else
master their greatness
laughing at the dreamers
because where I'm from
there's not a lot that make it
then when you become
an independent artist
you get viewed as
basic
local
fake shit
if they can't eat off your plate
supporting you is pointless
now you can let that shit
break you or make you
either way it's painful
take the bitter with the sweet
stay humble and thankful
grind for what you believe in
stay true to you
My Koncrete Jewels

~Purpose~

You had to be there,
to understand the words
she writes
if you truly knew her
you wouldn't question
the words she writes
The pen is her shield
the ink creates bloody bullets
her delivery is her gun
her mind is her trigger
and don't you dare her to pull it.
Weapon of mass destruction
were you hoping for a malfunction?
I'm sorry baby
this mental wasn't designed
for break downs
or shake downs
but created to achieve
until the next
generation
Believes
That they are great
And it's true
They will
Make mistakes
But learn from them
And do better
Because
The only way
To make your

Parent's proud
Is to Have
your shit Together

~Ask Wisely~

Don't ask me for shit
Because I don't have shit
To give
Now you be the judge
Am I speaking positive
Or negative
Because if I told you
You weren't shit
Some of you
Would be in your Feelings
But if I told you with a smile
"you the shit"
It would sound More appealing
And you'll accept the label
Just as everything else they bring
To the table
because you don't see
the difference
the things we accept
versus the things we reject
isn't that much different
no matter how much
we claim it to be
your shit will never smell like roses
but the right shit
will allow roses to grow
Beautifully
so don't ask me for shit
Because I don't have
Shit to give
And if you weren't Clear

from the Beginning
I am speaking Positive
And what I can give you
Are the tools to live
The fuel to drive
The word to give.

~Liars~

She says she hates liars
yet she loves herself
I guess her lies are "truths"
and her "truths"
are hidden well
currently in plain sight
but she thinks no one sees
it's hard to hide a lie
once it grows feet
but she hates liars
I swear that
hypocritical shit
irks me every time
because I know damn well
these hypocrites never document
their own crime
but will point out
yours and mine
we're condemned
for wearing a truth
everyone else would rather hide
condemned for speaking a truth
because some folks are more content
living their lie
liars, lie when they don't have too
you gave the truth yet one asked you
they hid a truth that was past due
now delayed
liars always say "it's better this way"
makes you wonder

does the Truth hurts
or do they need to save face
liars will tell you everything
but the truth
some will accept all but a lie
from someone else
if you listen close
you'll never hear a liar say
they hate themselves

~Round the Table~

Lemonade & Laughter
As we share our version
Of happily ever after
How it should be at the table
but nowadays broads
rather throw shade
ignorantly behave
blind to positive days
so they sit and lurk
checking on what the
next bitch has to say
who she pregnant by?
who's she is fucking
with today
who her man fucking
and what bills getting paid
a grown ass woman
doing childish things
kids have more "daddies"
than she has rings

out here "bad bitching"
worrying about the wrong things
plan b taking
because your priorities are insane
you're a have fun now
worry later kinda chick
out here doing reckless shit
but ya weave is lit
still in the PJs but ya whip is sick
some wonder is it worth it
out here dying to be perfect
that reflection must be unbearable
because you don't care if you hurt it
all that makeup conceals
is a beautiful face deserted
sitting round the table
like shit is perfect
fronting on purpose
forced interactions
provide temporary
satisfaction or distractions
so you begin to choose
encounters wisely
or not at all
texts replace phone calls
instead of simply
revealing motives
and hidden truths
dispelling rumors
and building groups
of strong sisters
we indirectly compete
front like shit is sweet

talk shit then retreat
mock another's defeat
criticize the same shit
being done behind
closed blinds
sisterhood comes at
a painful price
make sure the price tag isn't worth more than
your life
be wise round the table
be wise

~No Filter~

Share your character
share your flaws
would those things
still open doors
post your infidelities
post your lies
let's see if your bullshit
can get a thousand likes
post your addictions
post your insecurities
let's see how many
choose to retweet
post your TRUTH
nowadays it's the opposite
of what we're posting
because the "winning" is in
the bragging and boasting
bullshit overloading
throwing shade and railroading
competing to be noticed for all the wrong shit
then get mad when you didn't
get the attention your ass was so
thirsty to get
some post to entertain
dropping laughs in their newsfeed
but the ones that post their cries
for help get mocked and judged
follower fingers won't budge
no repost then
scroll on by

because we're not real-life friends
so post and don't judge
or judge and don't post
and stop worrying about
who is "doing the most"
cause honey it's some days
your similarities show
but of course
that's the selfie
you don't post

~Life Food~

Life food
Some have Been on
a thousand Diets
And still Haven't found
the "right food"
Because they don't truly
Know thy self
Your body doesn't
release
What the next person
Digests
so create your own Regrets
Or prevent Your own mistakes
But let the next person
Finish all that they
Have put on their plate

~ One Day~

One Day you will decide to
speak the truth
to those who have
heard your lies
for far too long
and no one will
want to listen
because when everyone
was requesting truth
you were bullshitting
too busy living your lie
to notice
your disrespectful
dispositions
People grew you didn't
moved on
you stayed still
now you're requesting
that someone else keeps it real
and hears you out
but attention
is all you care about
One Day
everyone will see you
for who you truly are
your reflection will bare
every one of your flaws
you won't stay protected
behind them closed doors
your Truth will be known
you shall Lie No more

~Truth~

Truth can be a Beautiful thing
It can also cause pain
Some embrace it
Some hide it deep in places
they think no one will ever look
Truth is deep on so many levels
because the parties involved
share so much
yet hide so much
at the same time
While one is accepting their own
the other may be concealing theirs
so they are not on the same wave
while one openly shares their own
they do not get the same in return
you could share a thousand
truths with someone
yet hide a thousand more
Some are big on the
Truth of others
yet serve the opposite
when it suits them
Some live their Truth at night
Others wear it proudly and loudly
The Time of day affects nothing
They're not afraid of
what others might see
Your Truth may offend others
Your Truth may inspire others
Your Truth may frighten others
Your Truth may hurt others

But it is your Truth
you must live it
whether you share it
with the world
or only a selected few
it is yours to LIVE!!!!

~Reckless Tendencies~

There I go, there I go, there I go
watching him walk away
with a part of me
that I didn't appreciate
because I easily gave it
to a stranger
who knows nothing more
than my first name
which is only an alias
I give until
I feel something deeper
than an orgasm
one would have to
truly be something
got me out here
sharing truths and shit
wanting to bare my soul
maybe even have some kids
One has yet to cross that bridge
but their sins have touched my lips
dirty hands have touched my hips
our demons dance under the moonlight
I'm aware many encounters
were not right
so I cleanse my soul
at midnight
There I go, there I go, there I go
watching him walk away
with my soul
promising that he'll return

I've learned the hard way
they'll say anything
until the doorway
touches their back
actions are unknown
during disappearing acts
actions are questioned
but they never provide facts
once a lie visits
the truth never returns
trust relocates
the heart will seek validation
until the brain confirms heartbreak.
There I go, there I go, there I go
watching him walk away
With someone else
It is now in this moment
that I am free
because I am no longer her
and she isn't me
maybe he'll provide her
with her own version
of happy
some would care to be
a fly on the wall
but I have saw
all that I needed
to see

~Apple Pie & Puffy Eyes~

Sometimes the things we long for
don't arrive in the form
of pie
as much as we hoped
it would make us
warm inside
it's a tortured ride
Our Pride
forces us to hide
behind the darkest shades
or the biggest smile
denying that life
and love has got
us down
have you ever sipped lemonade
under an apple tree
pretended to enjoy the breeze
unbothered by the bumble bees
because they provide honey
when the world provides shit
appreciate the beauty
never question it
oh, how the things
we want
don't come in the form
of pie
there will be times
when we will
find a thief
after we have scratched a lie

that painful truth
never makes us
feel warm inside
so we close
our eyes
and enjoy the ride

~Scorned ~

there isn't much you can say
to a woman scorned
your words
cannot undo the actions
her heart is torn
your apology means nothing
in the path of her rage
you wouldn't need to apologize
had you not misbehaved
yet there you are
verbally trying to make up
for your physical disrespect
sexual encounters
with strangers
who now create debt
how do you apologize
to watered eyes
that trusted you
do you admit your truths?
or simply reveal
a selected few
it isn't much you can say
to a woman
who has heard it all
saw it twice
and watched it fall
because he didn't know
what he had
and she only wanted
to give him her all

~Impress Me~

Offer me something
that I cannot find
within myself
And then we'll talk
until then
Admire me from your position
Until you're able to make
strong decisions
I want that concrete love
Not that quick attention
I need a man making moves
Not pimp decisions
If you feel I'm being rude
Pardon my honesty
But honestly
I'm just letting you know
what it takes to get
have and keep me
smiling that is
Because a woke woman
is never kept
She allows you
to enjoy her mystery
If you're lucky
the two of you
Will make history
But we must
create life first
After already making me
your wife first

If that's not something
you seek
then allow me to
say goodbye first.

~Dynamic Duo~

Let's make hearts melt
heads turn
Sheeps awaken
and souls burn
I'm talking about
You and I
giving the world
something so fly
Birth consciousness
so that negativity can die
I'd give you my last pen
Truly be your "write or die"
Let me know when you're
Ready to touch the sky

~The Other Side Of Visitation~

until you have been on the
other side of visitation
you could never
understand
a parent's frustration
with the court system
them judges, them lawyers,
those caseworkers
don't give a fuck
they don't get paid
to listen
just distribute
division
some are only
in that position
for the bag
they could truly
care less
about what's best
for your children
and your babies
don't understand
why things are now
different
so you try to explain
in the best way
as tears roll
down your face
Praying that
God is listening

until you have been
on the other side
of visitation
you will never
understand that hell
watching your children
grow
from a jail cell
1-hour visits
on a day you
never want to end
do you remember
how hard
it was saying good bye
to your best friend
imagine saying
good bye
to your children
hoping and praying
you'll see them
again
or leaving
one behind
because
you cannot take
both
the thought alone
burns my
fucking soul
could you imagine
losing the only
person

you wanted to live for
giving 1 hour
visitation
and a 20 minute
phone call
and you are not even
behind bars
just forced
to go through life
without
your baby girl
feeling like it's you
against the world
how the fuck
could the courts
prevent a father
that wants to do
right his child
from doing so
I guess we'll never know
of course
there is never
an explanation
during black family separations

~All aboard~

On the realest ride
you'll ever take in your life
these men are going to
sell your children
and rape your wife
that's not the half of it
they'll gloat with pride
while you raise their
bastard kids
after they've erased
your native tongue
and applied a name that fits
they will throw you in the fields
so you can pick their crops and shit
get outta line once
master pulls out his whip
100 lashes across your back
soon you realize
there's no way back
the place you called home
no longer exists
there are people here
who look just like you
but do not consider you
one of their own
not realizing
it's levels to this shit
Africa is also
their home
only difference is

they got here
a few years before you did
and they endured the same shit
you just did
and their fathers also
raised those bastard kids
the lighter ones still
weren't acknowledged
as master's kids
in the house preparing meals
for masters Bitch
and the name fits well
since she shows no shame
while sipping her lemonade
muting the cries
from inflicted pain
Imagine that
imagine our people
heard all that shit
and were able to turn back

~What If~

What if our president was still black
Our communities never saw crack
Martin lived to see his dream
Become a reality
and Coretta got her King back
What if Betty Shabazz
wouldn't have seen
that ultimate act of disrespect
where would we be
as a people
if Malcolm X
wasn't dead
what if the bullets
were never made
that filled so many guns
that caused
so many mothers
to bury their sons
what if the father
that wants to be there
gets to be there
without restriction
maybe then courts
could apply
the right convictions

~ Dying For The Wrong Shit~

Dying for recognition
always in competition
never willing to listen
to those feeding
their mental
with knowledge
instead they brag about the bullshit
you are talking about drugs and chains
I'm talking about nooses and whips
you complain on a crowded bus
imagine how many people
were on those ships
you know the ones
handled by the ones
whose drugs you flip
the same ones who will lock you up
when a new jail is built
but instead of standing with me
you'd rather stand against me
on some jealous shit
that's why we'll never be
what we're meant to be
because we can't agree on shit
it's better to divide
because unity
conquers shit
a lot of you are soldiers
straight up
you're just out here dying
for the wrong shit

dying to be seen
dying to be known
dying for a damn iPhone
dying for them new j's
or the latest foams
do you realize
how many died
because they wanted
to go home
wanted to be free
wanted to read
wanted to write
restricted from
simply enjoying
life
we take for granted
everything our ancestors
lived, died and marched for
and if we're not careful
the next generation
will take for granted
much more
always be clear
about everything
you're living, dying and fighting for
appreciate the day
use it
to right your wrongs

~Be Better~

You are guaranteed to be counted out
before you are counted in
from the moment
you are conceived
you are viewed as a sin
another n*gg*r born
out of wedlock
is what they assume
it doesn't matter
if your father
was present
the world still
expects less of you
prison cells
have already
been designed
with you in mind
as well as the laws
they are expecting
you to break
before you reach 29
that is
if you see 18
reach 21
get your first job
have your first son
the law is counting on
your downfall
so stand tall
and live right
be wise

with your fights
the goal is to be
better than
they expected
the goal is
keep them cells
empty
the goal is
to have a masterplan
how can you
how will you
do better
be better
and stay better
how will you
help the next brother
get his shit together
because the more
the better
and I rather see
a thousand brothers
doing right
than a thousand brothers
doing wrong
providing free labor
for the state
but when they come home
the same state
that benefited off that
free labor
is not fucking with them
never realizing
that's part of the

scheme
there's not enough
to keep you out
but it's more than
enough
to get you in
keep you in
separated
from family and friends
this shit is designed
to break you
Black Man
walk down the wrong path
and one shall
find cuffs near his hands
as if he truly
had golden opportunities
you and I both know
the only gold
some black folks
know is
the grillz
we put on our
teeth
because the hype
is to look rich
rocking
ridiculous shit
borrowing from
another broke
mother fucker
to impress someone
whose credit score
is bullshit

that's what we're doing
in 2018
the progression
is in fake flexing
over stretching
that barely earned dollar
popping tags, p*$$y and collars
makes your ancestors
wanna holla
what the fuck
are you thinking
you are an embarrassment
to every black man
that marched
for you
front lawn was torched
for you
fought for things
you refuse to
appreciate
I know the lessons life
sometimes provide aren't easy
but it's imperative
that you graduate
do more than
make your parents proud
create a life
proudly for your child
for that child
will be left in the world
you leave them in
whether you realize it
or not

how you contributed
to this world
will affect them
Be Better!

~For My People~

Another one gone
as we watch the media in anger
the family mourns
a child is without a father
a mother must bury her son
We shouldn't have to say
Black lives matter
because we all should be
treated with respect
but it's evident
the darker your skin
the more you face neglect.
We had our hands up
asking you to not shoot
after Mike Brown
I was afraid to let my son's
travel alone
the way they let Zimmerman
put Trayvon down
no respect for life
look how they handled Freddie
and we're still asking for justice
when we should have
been getting ready
because when brother Garner
told them he couldn't breath
they took his last breath anyway
it was time for action
anytime, anyplace, anywhere
it could happen

a sister was found hanging
in a cell she shouldn't have been in
due to the color of her skin
she was stopped and assaulted
never seen alive again
we're still being easy
we're still being quiet
some even assume
the solution is a riot
there is no solution
for this injustice
on constant repeat
let's start with a financial defeat
then move on
to conquer together
maybe then
we'll ruffle some feathers
and they will get their shit together
our young brothers and sisters
will have the chance
to do better, see better and be better
until then
this is an open letter
We, The grandchildren
of the Africans you stole
are asking that you
let that grudge go
we get it
we're stronger
and you can't handle defeat
so you created laws to feel superior
and groom us like sheep

gave your grandsons
badges and guns
to shoot us down in the streets
dirty hands are never clean
when the sins
are on repeat

~C.R.A.C.K~

You were created to weaken
the people
you couldn't control
manipulated brothers
to sell their soul
sisters selling their body
for the pipe
they never realize
those chains are for life
dreams turn into nightmares
destroyed bonds between peers
the thirst is always stronger than
the wrong committed to quench it
so many guilty parties
but only our brothers and sisters
are sentenced
everybody got a cut,
everybody benefited from your bullshit
except for the children of the parents
you left at death's door

www.ingramcontent.com/pod-product-compliance
Lightning Source LLC
Chambersburg PA
CBHW071648040426
42452CB00009B/1809